DR. MELROSE BETHEA

DIVINE
Interruptions

GOD'S INVITATION TO DRAW NEAR TO HIM

God's Life
PUBLISHING
HAWAII   NEW JERSEY

Divine Interruptions
by Melrose Bethea

Published by:
God's Life Publishing
5369 Edgewater Dr. Ewa Beach, HI 96706
Email: godlife@aol.com

Web: www.godslifepublishing.org

Designed by: God's Life Publishing

Cover Design: Calvin L. Bethea

ISBN: 978-1-950315-10-7
Printed in the United States of America

God's Life
PUBLISHING

Dedication

This book is dedicated to the Author and Finisher of my faith, the Lord Jesus Christ who has purchased my wretched life from utter destruction. All the honor, all the glory and all the praises are due unto your Holy Name.

Thank you Holy Spirit for directing and translating into words the mind of God concerning divine interruptions. Without you these pages would have remained empty.

May each reader lay it to heart the depth of the Father's love to continually draw him or her to Himself especially during divine interruptions in our plans.

Acknowledgments

I would like to thank Min. Margaret Adjoga-Otu, for her unwavering dedication in proofreading, and providing feedback concerning this work.

Special thanks to Min. Shamika Simmons for her tireless prayers and excitement every step of the way.

To my mom, Josephine Havas, who accepted the divine interruption in her life to allow God to use her body as a place of preparation for my birth.

And to my husband, Bishop Calvin L. Bethea, thank you for your support, continued confidence in my obedience to God's will, your prayers and coaching to see this book to its completion.

Finally, I give thanks to all the prayer partners that have stood in the gap and prayed for me while I was going through my numerous divine interruptions.

CONTENT

PREFACE

Jesus warned us that before His return, we would see the signs of the times all around us. Wars and rumors of wars, pestilence, famine, natural disasters and men loving themselves more than loving God. As a result, many people are struggling daily with numerous interruptions in their lives. It is causing their hearts to fail. Depression is at an all-time high, suicidal thoughts are rampant, and hopelessness has captivated many individuals. Some play the blame game, even blaming God. Truly, God should be the last person we should have issues with. The things that are happening in our lives are not sent by God for our destruction but are a tool used by God to draw us near to Him.

I have had many divine interruptions in my life, especially when I became a Christian in 1989. Before Christ, I thought I had the perfect plan for my life. I was going to complete medical school, do a surgical residency and launch a private practice all before I was thirty-three years old. Continuing on my wonderful plan, I was going to get married and begin a family when I was thirty-five years old. Nevertheless, five months before I began Podiatric Medical School, I repented of my sins and accepted Jesus Christ as my personal Lord and Savior.

My first divine interruption was in my third year of medical school when I got married at the age of twenty-seven to a spirit-filled man of God with a calling to teach believers their identity in Christ. I was supportive of him until the next divine interruption came along. One night in prayer, the Spirit of the Lord spoke to me about helping my husband to build a church. This was a real challenge since I was not raised in the church, had no knowledge of what a pastor's wife was supposed to do and did not know anything about planting a church. God was yet holding my hand and reminding me that His ways were not my ways. Be still He whispered, "*I am God*".

I experienced another divine interruption, when the Lord spoke to me during my fourth year of medical school and told me that He would call me His physician before man called me a doctor. I was panic-stricken. Leaning to my own understanding, I thought I would need to read the whole Bible and memorize parts of it before graduation. As a result, I resolved to do so during commuting to school every day, taking one bus and two trains from New Jersey to New York. On the train, I would often have my pocket Bible in one hand, while holding onto the hang straps with the other as I read. God was at work; using these situations to cause me to become a student of the Word, grow my faith in Him, and transform me into His daughter.

Many more divine interruptions would

come. We lost our home and were homeless for a year while pastoring the church. During this time, I developed our children's church ministry, established a worship team and became the administrator for our church. I would minister on divine healing in Nigeria, Africa; minister the Word in Jamaica, West Indies as well as Hawaii and other venues. God's thoughts towards me were not evil. It was all designed to bring the best out of me for Him.

As a result of my numerous divine interruptions, God was able to prepare me to be a proper help meet for my husband in marriage and ministry. He gave me over thirty children who affectionately call me mom. Divine interruptions were God's methods to redirect, instruct and order my steps to experience His expected end for each season of my life. The person who is not born again may not see God's hand at work and only view these challenges as a crisis. However, the deviations in my plans were only a tool to fulfill God's divine plan for my life. The Devil was not the cause or the facilitator of the events that took me away from my plans. It was all God. These divine interruptions were not meant to punish me for some unknown sin or cause me to rush and find a quick fix without regard of the invisible hand of the Almighty. Every divine interruption that I have experienced has worked for my good and has brought glory to God. Even in co-writing this book, I had a divine interruption. One day when I was approximately ninety-eight percent complete, the entire document turned into asterisks. Only a previous document was available and about ten hours of work was permanently lost. Truly, *"all things work together for good to them that love God, to them who are called according to his purpose"* (Romans 8:28).

INTRODUCTION

Many of us can quote the 23rd Psalms, but have never asked ourselves what the phrase, *"he leadeth me beside the still waters"* means (Psalm 23:2b). As I began to ponder this phrase, Holy Spirit began to share with me that God allows divine interruptions in our lives to lead us by still waters. This means that God is present with us in our troubles, leading us on the course that avoids the boisterous waves while holding our hand during the storms of life. When an unsaved person is faced with trouble, he or she only has the ability to view and respond to it as a crisis. A crisis by their definition is a time of intense difficulty, trouble or danger that requires a quick decision. Therefore, a person without Christ is more prone to take matters into his or her own hands and become mister or misses fix it. Until Christ is allowed to remove the scales from the sinner's eyes, he or she cannot view their trouble as a work of God. On the other hand, a born again Christian views trouble as a work of God to redirect his or her life towards the pre-ordained expected end. When God is allowed to do the leading, our crucial situation will be embraced as a divine interruption that will lead us on a path to ultimate discovery of our Heavenly Father. Christians experience divine interruptions, while sinners can only experience their difficulty as a crisis.

We are so bent on desiring to lead ourselves that God has to interrupt our plans in order for us to yield to His will. Sometimes, we have been stubborn and stiff-necked like the children of Israel. Consequently, only an interruption in our plans will cause us to look to our Creator. God doesn't desire us to be in the turbulent seas of our challenge. However, He does desire us to reconnect with Him and walk in the peace of His presence.

Initially, it may seem as if an obstacle that we are experiencing is going to destroy us. However, if allowed to serve its purpose, the disruption has the ability to cause us to reconnect or begin a new relationship with our Heavenly Father through His Son, Jesus Christ. The difficulty ultimately becomes the doorway, enabling us to step out of mediocrity and into the supernatural blessings of God. Jesus said, "I am the door of the sheep" (see **John 10:7, 9**). It is through Jesus Christ that the unsaved can go from having a troublesome crisis to a joyous divine interruption experience.

It is my aim to encourage you, while you are going through your divine interruption to become focused on Christ. The best will come, even if it currently makes no sense. Your trouble is a small detour that will lead to great blessings. God loves you and will give you grace to endure the challenges that confront you. His thoughts towards you are not evil. God made it clear to the prophet Jeremiah, who suffered many things and had calamity after calamity. "For I know the thoughts that I think toward you, saith the Lord, thoughts of peace, and not of evil, to give you an expected end" (**Jeremiah 29:11**). You have a Heavenly Father, who will hold your hand and lead you through the valley of the shadow of death, so you can walk with confidence in His love. Ultimately, your divine interruption will guide you to the perfect will of God.

1

CHAPTER ONE

DIVINE

INTERRUPTION

*"A man's heart deviseth his way:
but the Lord directeth his steps"*

(Proverbs 16:9)

King Solomon was recorded in the scriptures as being the wisest man to have lived. His wisdom came from God and not from the counselors around his court. He learned the hard way by the many mistakes he made in pursuing his plans with the women of his choosing. At the end of his days, King Solomon confessed that all his plans amounted to nothing simply because he did not allow the Lord to direct his steps. They were all vanity (see **Ecclesiastes 1:2**).

"What we are so quick to call a crisis is often nothing more than a divine interruption in our lives."

No one appreciates the interruption of a well-planned event. In fact, most would rather their plans come to pass just as they had envisioned. Many of us are so prone to define trying times in our lives based on our five senses, that it rarely occurs to us that there is a spiritual underlying reason. When such times occur, it is quite natural to express how we don't like it, don't want it, and don't wish to change as a result of it! What we are so quick to call a crisis is often nothing more than a divine interruption in our lives. Collins English Dictionary defines an interruption as the following: *"something such as an action, comment, or question, that causes someone or something to stop or change course in the midst of what they were doing"*. While on this road called life, many will find themselves in one divine interruption after another. The sole purpose of these events is to lead you to a deeper commitment to Jesus Christ.

No matter where you are in your relationship with the Lord Jesus Christ, interruptions are an invitation to draw nearer to Him.

C. S. Lewis, the British writer and lay theologian had this to say concerning divine interruption: *"The great thing, if one can, is to stop regarding all the unpleasant things as interruptions of one's 'own,' or 'real' life. The truth is of course that what one calls the interruptions are precisely one's real life -- the life God is sending one day by day."* Though some would disagree with C. S. Lewis, his point is valid. The disruption of your plans cause you to experience the fullness of the life God planned for you. It is through these unpleasant experiences that God stops your forward momentum, changes your direction and redirect you to follow His course.

Let us ponder this for a moment. Opportunities to connect with God and our family are almost nonexistent in today's society. Often times, we are so busy with the hustle and bustle of daily living that we miss the true experiences of life. Busy, busy, busy is what we are known for. This ought not be so. We can run to our car yet never notice the trees, birds, and flowers, or look up into the sky. Even coffee drinkers are in such a rush that they don't have time to smell the coffee. A crisis is more than the panic and fear that we are so quick to recognize. It can be the ultimate means by which God visits you in an effort to draw you back into His divine will. God will allow events to occur in your life in order to instruct or redirect you. Seeking and pursuing a relationship with Him is His ultimate goal for each of us.

God desires to bless his people; however the blessings will not be realized until we embrace our perceived crisis as a vehicle of divine interruption to transform us into a proper relationship with God. The blessings did not come to the many servants of God in the Bible until they allowed the observed crisis to be the tool that brought an interruption in their comfort zones that produced tremendous blessings in their lives.

If you were beginning to say to yourself that no one is facing a terrible predicament like me, please consider the following. Elijah the prophet thought that he was the only one who was facing a life threatening set back when the evil Jezebel sought to take his life. He realized that he was clearly wrong when the Lord told him that there were 7,000 faithful servants whose knees had not bowed to Baal (see **1 Kings 19:18**). You are not the only one in a strait.

Look at some of the recorded divine interruptions that many in the Bible faced.

-**Abraham** had a heavy heart when he was told by God to sacrifice Issac, his only son (see **Genesis 22:1-14**).

-**Jacob** was troubled when he escaped by night from Laban's house into the revengeful arms of Esau, his brother. Who previously made a vow to kill him (see **Genesis 31:1-18, 32:9-11**).

-**Moses** was perplexed when he saw the burning

bush and God told him to go to Pharaoh and tell him to let His people go. Obedience to God's command could mean Moses' death (see **Exodus 3:1-10**).

-**Jonah** was in a quandary when he was commissioned to go and preach to Nineveh of their coming destruction. They were a people he hated and wanted God to destroy. Knowing the mercy of God, Jonah knew God would not destroy them, and refused to go to Nineveh (see **Jonah chapters 1-4**).

-**Shadrach, Meshach and Abednego** had a confrontation with King Nebuchadnezzar when they refused to bow to the golden image and faced a fiery furnace (see **Daniel 3:14-21**).

-**Daniel** had a death sentence when he violated the king's decree, and prayed to Jehovah. As a result, he was placed in a den of lions (see **Daniel 6:10-16**).

-**Ruth** had a separation when she decided to leave her family and culture to follow her mother-in-law to Bethlehem after both their husbands died (see **Ruth 1:16-19**).

-The fishermen **(Peter, Andrew, James & John)** left their comfort zone when Jesus told them to leave their family businesses and follow Him (see **Matthew 4:18-20**).

-**Jairus** had a delay when Jesus was on his way to his home to heal his dying daughter and was interrupted by a woman with an issue of blood (see **Mark 5: 21-42**).

-**Peter** was distraught when he denied Jesus three times and the cock crowed (see **John 18:15-27**).

-**Saul of Tarsus** attention was arrested when he was blinded on the road to Damascus, while seeking to persecute Christians (see **Acts 9:1-8**).

"God has a larger purpose that will bring blessings to us as well as others, when we accept His redirection and guidance."

-**The Philippian jailer** had a distressing emergency when God miraculously opened the jail cells of all the prisoners (see **Acts 16:25-27**).

-**Personally**, I had a divine interruption, when God told me to close my podiatry practice and help my husband build the church.

Everyone mentioned above had a supernatural visitation that unveiled their eyes and redirected their steps to the path God wanted them to follow. These circumstances were not for their destruction but for their instruction. As a result, each of these servants developed a closer relationship with God.

The ultimate lesson here is for us to embrace whatever interruption we are confronted with regardless of how it blocks our plans. God has a larger purpose that will bring blessings to us as well as others, when we accept His redirection and guidance.

Set your eyes on the scriptures below, and allow them to cause you to hold on to God's hand so that He will lead and guide you into His blessings.

Psalm 61:2 *"From the end of the earth will I cry unto thee, when my heart is overwhelmed: lead me to the rock that is higher than I".*

Psalm 119:133 *"Order my steps in thy word: and let not any iniquity have dominion over me".*

Proverbs 15:22 *"Without counsel purposes are disappointed: but in the multitude of counsellors they are established".*

Proverbs 19:21 *"There are many devices in a man's heart; nevertheless the counsel of the Lord, that shall stand".*

Isaiah 55:8 *"For my thoughts are not your thoughts, neither are your ways my ways, saith the Lord".*

Jeremiah 29:11 *"For I know the thoughts that I think toward you, saith the Lord, thoughts of peace, and not of evil, to give you an expected end".*

Prayer and confession for divine interruptions in your life:

"Heavenly Father, I thank you that you have a plan to prosper and protect my life, give me peace and an expected end. Thank you for allowing divine interruptions in my life to draw me back into your plan for my life. I

acknowledge that your ways are not my ways and your thoughts are not my thoughts. I ask for forgiveness for being blinded to the purpose of your redirection for my life. Enable me through the power of the Holy Spirit to obey and accept your plan for my life. Amen."

2

CHAPTER TWO

CONNECT WITH GOD

"Casting all your care upon him;
for he careth for you"

(1 Peter 5:7)

Either a divine interruption will be approached from a spiritual standpoint or from a non-spiritual perspective. Christians will tend to apply a spiritual solution, which is to turn to Christ and the Holy Scriptures. The non-Christian doesn't have Christ as their source; therefore, he or she will seek to handle a delay of their plans using non-Biblical methods. These include leaning to their own understanding and following the recommendations of the world. Since all divine interruptions are out of an individual's control, it would seem logical for us to look to a source who is in control and greater than man. That source and answer is Jesus Christ. If you have tried everything that you know to fix your divine interruption and are still afflicted, then I offer you Jesus.

"If you have tried everything that you know to fix your divine interruption and are still afflicted, then I offer you Jesus".

The Apostle Peter penned these words as instruction: *"Casting all your care upon him; for he careth for you"* (1 Peter 5:7). The instructions to cast your cares upon Christ demonstrates an active posture in how we are to present our concerns or burdens to the Lord. God cares for your soul and has made provisions through Christ's death, burial and resurrection to fix your sin problem. Simply ask God to forgive your sin, be willingly to turn from your sin and accept the work of Christ on the cross. Jesus came to redeem you and be a bridge to restore your relationship with the Father. Once your sin issue is settled, you will have Holy Spirit and the whole host of heaven to help you in every area of your life.

The Apostle Peter states that, *"in time past we were not a people, but are now the people of God:"* (1 Peter 2:10). Becoming the people of God is not just God's work. We also have to do our part by agreeing with God that He has given us the means by which we can become a new creature. There is a well-known story recorded in the Bible about the requirements to become a child of God. Nicodemus was facing a critical time in his life. He struggled with what he should do with Jesus' teaching versus what he had been taught. He was a well-trained religious teacher of the Mosaic Law. He decided to visit Jesus at night to inquire about the miracles Jesus had done. Nonetheless, Nicodemus was perplexed when Jesus told him, *"you must be born again"* (see John 3:1-9). Clearly no one can go back into his or her mother's womb and be reborn. This only proves that education in religious matters is insufficient to understand what Jesus was saying. To be "born again" or to receive salvation is deliverance from sin and its consequences, brought about by faith in Jesus Christ. Salvation is not a physical experience. It is a spiritual transformation that results in a new birth, producing eternal life and membership into the family of God. We are now officially the people of God when we respond to Holy Spirit drawing us to the Father and repenting of our sin. We will no longer have to battle any unplanned detours without help from the God who made the heavens and the earth.

Every single person born after the fall of Adam and Eve in the Garden of Eden has a sinful nature. In Romans 3:23, we learn that, *"All have sinned and come short of the glory of God".* This text is straightforward and to the point; all have sinned! Contrary to what many in the world believe, God is still holy. Because of His holiness He cannot embrace sin. Therefore, our sin nature and the sins that we commit separate us from God or creates a disconnect or wedge between us and God. The above scripture says all have sinned, not some, not a few - but all. All is an inclusive term, encompassing everyone, living everywhere in the earth. If you have borrowed anything without permission, desired something that belonged to someone else, lied to protect your job or image, entertained evil thoughts, pretended blind or ignorant to an event you witnessed; then you my friend have sinned. In the Bible, sin is defined as a transgression of the law of God (see **1 John 3:4** and rebellion against God (see **Deuteronomy 9:7, Joshua 1:18**). The only remedy for sin is repentance followed by the acceptance of Jesus Christ as your (personal)Lord and Savior (see **Romans 10:9**). Based on the previous paragraphs, if you realize that you have never asked Jesus to forgive you for your sin, then use the sample prayer below as a primer to help you connect with God.

Prayer and confession to connect with Jesus Christ as your Savior:

"God, I come to you in the name of your dear son Jesus Christ, I acknowledge that I have sinned against you and brought great pain and sadness in my life. I ask you to forgive me of all my sins. I choose to forgive those that have hurt me because I seek your forgiveness. I ask you to renew my mind as I read and study the Holy Scriptures. I now invite you to come live in me, help me to please you and guide me to walk in your truth. I thank you for inviting me to begin a new relationship with you. I accept all the benefits of your invitation now. I confess that I am no longer a sinner but a child of God. Thank you for saving me from eternal damnation and restoring my relationship with you. I choose today to daily appreciate and walk in this wonderful gift of salvation. In Jesus name, Amen."

Congratulations to you if you have prayed this prayer in sincerity. Now, you have a new identity in Christ. Our identity encompasses who we are, the way we think about ourselves, and the way the world or others view us. We often identify people by their physical appearance (height, hair color or length, complexion), or by the kind of employment they have (policeman, teacher, administrator, physician, plumber, mechanic), or by their denomination affiliation (Baptist, Assembly of God, Presbyterian, Pentecostal).

Though we want to agree with God, we have an adversary who faithfully works to blind and block us from accepting our new nature in Christ. We sometimes work harder at the title others give us or by the label we give ourselves, rather than placing emphasis on our relationship with and to God. In the Apostle Paul's letter to the church at Corinth, he reminds the new converts that, *"... if any man be in Christ, he is a new creature: old things are passed away; behold, all things are become new"* (2 Corinthians 5:17). God already defined you! Moreover, He desires you to agree with Him by defining yourself according to your spiritual identity as a child of God. You can learn more about your new identity by reading the Bible daily. Furthermore, you are a new creature; old things and labels are passed away. You are not who you used to be. You were a sinner, but now you are a saint. You were a liar, but now you are a faithful witness who does not lie (see **Proverbs 14:5**). No longer are you identified by your physical appearance. Your spiritual position in Christ now identifies you! You are a Christian; a follower of Jesus Christ. According to Ephesians chapter one, you are now chosen, holy, without blame, adopted, accepted in the beloved, redeemed, forgiven, filled with wisdom and prudence and sealed with the Holy Spirit of promise.

Before you surrendered your life to Christ's lordship, there was a way you handled whatever challenges came your way. Perhaps, you may have been one that sought comfort in "comfort foods". In your panic, you may have called all your friends looking for answers. Maybe, you might have turned to the bottle, pills, or pornography. Possibly, you may have even kept a watchful and listening ear to the radio or television in hope of some good news. You might have developed other means of escaping your reality. Now that you are in Christ, however,

God requires you to walk in your new identity as a Christian. It is in seeking first the kingdom (see **Matthew 6:33**) of God, that there will be a breakthrough or deliverance from your predicament. Your relationship with Christ will determine how soon the peace of God will come over you or how soon the fearful thoughts in your head will overwhelm you.

Although you are a new creature in Christ (see **2 Corinthians 5:17**), at times you may still think and feel the same way you did before you received Christ as your personal savior. Why? Everything you learned before you knew Christ is still programmed into your memory. Because there is no mental delete button, you may sometimes still think and perceive the situation according to the ways of the old person. Every memory, attitude, mannerism, perception, value system, or preference did not die overnight. You must work at being transformed by the renewing of your mind. It has often been said that twenty-one consecutive days of doing the same thing will create a habit of that thing in your life. That is why the Apostle Paul said, *"And be not conformed to this world, but be ye transformed by the renewing of your mind"* (Romans 12:2). Your mind must be renewed by the word of God so that you will say and think about yourself, what God has already spoken about the new you.

Below are scriptures on which to meditate. The psalmist made it clear that, *"the entrance of thy words giveth light; it giveth understanding unto the simple"* (Psalm 119:130). When you are able to look at the word of God and repeat it out loud to yourself, your outlook will be more confident. You will also have a bold assurance that God will deliver you. Faith comes by hearing and hearing the word of God (see **Romans 10:17**).

So go ahead and **repeat these verses of scripture aloud.**

Psalm 32:7 *"Thou art my hiding place; thou shalt preserve me from trouble; thou shalt compass me about with songs of deliverance"*.

Psalm 73:26 *"My flesh and my heart faileth: but God is the strength of my heart, and my portion for ever"*.

John 1:12 *"But as many as received him, to them gave he power to become the sons of God, even to them that believe on his name:"*

John 6:47 *"Verily, verily, I say unto you, He that believeth on me hath everlasting life"*.

John 16:33 *"These things I have spoken unto you, that in me ye might have peace. In the world ye shall have tribulation: but be of good cheer; I have overcome the world"*.

Romans 5:8 *"But God commendeth his love toward us, in that, while we were yet sinners, Christ died for us"*.

Romans 6:23 *"For the wages of sin is death; but the gift*

of God is eternal life through Jesus Christ our Lord".

Romans 10:9 *"That if thou shalt confess with thy mouth the Lord Jesus, and shalt believe in thine heart that God hath raised him from the dead, thou shalt be saved".*

2 Corinthians 5:21 *"For he hath made him to be sin for us, who knew no sin; that we might be made the righteousness of God in him".*

2 Corinthians 5:17 *"Therefore if any man be in Christ, he is a new creature: old things are passed away; behold, all things have become new".*

Prayer and confession to cast your cares on the Lord during an interruption of your plans:

"Father, forgive me for allowing my difficulties to cause my flesh and heart to fail. Thank you for showing me grace and mercy when I rejected you and leaned to my own understanding. I confess with my mouth and believe in my heart that I will be saved from all of my troubles. I choose today to cast my cares upon Christ because He cares for me.
Amen."

3

CHAPTER THREE

CHRIST IN YOUR DIVINE INTERRUPTION

"We are troubled on every side, yet not distressed; we are perplexed, but not in despair; Persecuted, but not forsaken; cast down, but not destroyed; Always bearing about in the body the dying of the Lord Jesus, that the life also of Jesus might be made manifest in our body"

(2 Corinthians 4:8-10).

The Apostle Paul faced character assassination
when false teachers swayed the church at Corinth
against him. In these verses, he implies that some
type of divine interruption will occur in the life
of every living person, especially those who are
believers in Christ. The same feelings or thoughts
the Apostle Paul was challenged with in this crucial
time will also be stirred in you when you face similar
challenges. Regardless of what the interruption is,
it will always elicit a similar array of emotions. He
stated that the difficulty he was in was connected to
his (commitment to Christ) and that it caused him to
be troubled, perplexed, persecuted and cast down.
Each of these words selected by the Apostle Paul was
carefully chosen to paint a picture of what his divine
interruption was like.

The Apostle Paul was troubled by problems
and conflicts that surrounded his relationship
with the church at Corinth. He was perplexed or
completely baffled and filled with uncertainty
regarding why they would embrace such lies
about his character. He faced persecution, which
manifested itself in hostility and ill treatment
because of religious lifestyle and beliefs. He was
consciously aware of being cast down or saddened
and worried about the situation. His peace, ministry
and life were being threatened.

Interruption Defined
Each of these words (troubled, perplexed, persecuted, cast down) describe many of the nuances that
convey what an interruption is. Let us define how an

interruption looks, feels and how it manifests itself. According to the New Oxford American Dictionary, *an interruption is an event that stops the continuous progress of an activity or process.* As a result, it triggers the feelings of fear and threat, which cause a sequence of unexpected events. It is a situation that causes a stressful time in an individual's life when they experience a breakdown or disruption in their usual or normal daily activities or family functioning. An interruption also involves any event that is expected to lead to an unstable and dangerous situation affecting an individual, group, community or whole society. Another characteristic of an interruption is that no one can predict the outcome.

You may not be undergoing a spiritual conflict because of your faith in Christ Jesus like the Apostle Paul. However, each of us may have experienced or might currently be experiencing an interruption that threatens our way of life, brings intense difficulty to us or positions us in physical danger. These may include but are not limited to the following: illness, unemployment, divorce, death of a loved one, substance abuse, viruses, plagues and wars. Though it may be difficult to see Christ in the midst of your trouble, He is yet there. He has promised not to leave or forsake you (see **John 13:33, Matthew 28:20**). During these times, it will be more apparent whether our hope and confidence is in the Lord Jesus Christ or something/someone else. If you view an interruption through the eyes of God, you will be more prone to see the hand of God working purpose in it. When you are not agreeing with whom God says you are, you are more likely to allow whatever predicament you're in to cause you to question your identity. A little voice inside may whisper to you,

"If you view an interruption through the eyes of God, you will be more prone to see the hand of God working purpose in it."

"If God loves you and you are a Christian, how come you are sick? How come you don't have any money? How come you are not being promoted on your job?"

Faith comes by hearing and hearing by the word of God. Satan cunningly whispers in the ears of believer's, "you are useless," "you are ugly," "you are fat" and other words and phrases that are contrary to the new man. He daily pursues trying to cause us to have "identity amnesia" whereby we forget who God has made us. When we are not careful or attentive to God's voice, we will repeat the lies Satan tells us. His voice will drown out the small still voice of Holy Spirit.

Nevertheless, let's explore various type of interruptions and how to deal with them God's way.

Types of Interruptions

There are numerous types of interruptions. For our purposes we will only look at a few to demonstrate the impact to the lives of individuals. These interruptions create countless emotions leading to all kinds of behavior that is not easily controlled apart from divine intervention.

A business interruption is an event that occurs suddenly and causes a disruption to the daily operations of a business. It is characterized by activities like illegal misconduct, leadership change, and bad customer service leading to a loss of revenue. This interruption leaves a person in wonderment. How come I didn't see this coming is always the question that is on the person's mind.

Workplace interruption involves the disruption of work by the employees of an organization. Examples include workplace violence, discrimination, and workers going on a strike, bullying and gossip. This type of interruption has a long-term influence and the ability to disturb the mental health of the employees of the organization. "I should have done so-and-so," is always the thought.

Technology interruption includes hardware failure, software compromise or an industrial accident (transformer expulsion, fire destroying equipment). The loss of e-mails, pictures, documents and personal data may become irretrievable. This type of interruption blocks a person's vision of positive thoughts about the future. It creates a feeling as if my life as I knew is over.

Natural interruptions are often referred to as "acts of God". No individual person is the cause. Examples of a natural interruption are volcano, earthquake, tsunami, torrential floods, avalanche, tornado, viruses or plagues. A search for someone to blame often comes up short.

A personal interruption is what it says it is personal. It is the inability for a person to adapt to change and solve personal problems. Examples of personal interruption are divorce, illness of self or a family member, unemployment, custody battle, robbery and sexual abuse. Though it may begin with one or two persons, it has the ability to impact many individuals. This type of interruption has the ability to cultivate a sense of emptiness.

All interruptions have the same fingerprint or identification patterns. They produce a fear of losing the life that you have become accustomed to. Moreover, they create a loss of focus, which overwhelms you with anxiousness and feelings of helplessness, making it hard for you to trust God. All of these fears are legitimate. They are not figments of your imagination. Adversities are real. Therefore, you have a real God who is over every difficulty that comes your way and will show you how to triumph in it. Through Christ the impossible will become possible and victory will be realized.

However, a major obstacle in getting over any interruption is the impulse of denial. To deny the abrupt discontinuity of your plan is to have a firm refusal that the disturbance exists or is true. Denial also resists the implications or claims of an interruption. Nevertheless, the Apostle Paul was not such a person who denied what he constantly faced. As quickly as he described the feelings that he had due to the interruption, he countered it with his hope in Christ. He affirmed I am not distressed, not in despair, not forsaken, and I am not destroyed because of this critical impasse. He acknowledged that this hardship was real, but it was for Jesus' sake, *"that the life also of Jesus might be made manifest in our mortal flesh"* (2 Corinthians 4:11). He also encouraged believers by saying, *"And not only so, but we glory in tribulations also: knowing that tribulation worketh patience; And patience, experience; and experience, hope: And hope maketh not ashamed; because the love of God is shed abroad in our hearts by the Holy Ghost which is given unto us"* (Romans 5:3-5).

Let's search the scriptures and **see who Jesus is in your divine interruption.**

Psalm 23 *"The Lord is my shepherd; I shall not want. He maketh me to lie down in green pastures: he leadeth me beside the still waters. He restoreth my soul: he leadeth me in the paths of righteousness for his name's sake. Yea, though I walk through the valley of the shadow of death, I will fear no evil: for thou art with me; thy rod and thy staff they comfort me. Thou preparest a table before me in the presence of mine enemies: thou anointest my head with oil; my cup runneth over. Surely goodness and mercy shall follow me all the days of my life: and I will dwell in the house of the Lord for ever".*

Matthew 11:28 *"Come unto me, all ye that labour and are heavy laden, and I will give you rest".*

Matthew 21:22 *"And all things, whatsoever ye shall ask in prayer, believing, ye shall receive".*

Luke 10:19 *"Behold, I give unto you power to tread on serpents and scorpions, and over all the power of the enemy: and nothing shall by any means hurt you".*

Luke 12:31-32 *"But rather seek ye the kingdom of God; and all these things shall be added unto you. Fear not, little flock; for it is your Father's good pleasure to give you the kingdom".*

John 8:12 *"Then spake Jesus again unto them, saying, I am the light of the world: he that followeth me shall not walk in darkness, but shall have the light of life".*

John 10:9 *"I am the door: by me if any man enter in, he shall be saved, and shall go in and out, and find pasture".*

John 14:26-27 *"But the Comforter, which is the Holy Ghost, whom the Father will send in my name, he shall teach you all things, and bring all things to your remembrance, whatsoever I have said unto you. Peace I leave with you, my peace I give unto you: not as the world giveth, give I unto you. Let not your heart be troubled, neither let it be afraid".*

John 15:7 *"If ye abide in me, and my words abide in you, ye shall ask what ye will, and it shall be done unto you".*

**Prayer and confession for Christ
in your interruption:**

"Father, I thank you that Jesus Christ is the Good Shepherd who never leaves me. I confess that Christ is my refuge and strength. I ask you to comfort, instruct and teach me the way I should go. I choose to abide in your words and plan for my life. Set my foot upon the right path so that I may run the race that you have set before me with all confidence that my past is behind me and cannot overtake me. In Jesus name Amen."

4

CHAPTER FOUR

ALL THINGS WORK TOGETHER FOR GOOD

"And we know that all things work together for good to them that love God, to them who are the called according to his purpose"

(Romans 8:28).

The Apostle Paul penned this verse while he was teaching the church at Rome about the power of Holy Spirit to aid and deliver the saints. Often many Christians quote this verse in a casual way. No deep thought is taken concerning what all things would encompass. This scripture is very powerful for whatever divine interruption you find yourself.

We don't mind that something's working for our good, especially if it's already a good thing. Nevertheless, all things can include potentially good things as well as bad things. How is it possible that something bad can be a good thing? The Apostle Paul must have truly lost his mind on this one! However, the implication here is that the interruption can be either an opportunity or a danger depending on one's perception about the situation. In other words, a bad thing can be a good thing in disguise. Losing one's job may be bad, but it is also an opportunity to get a better paying job with better benefits. Failing the medical board exam may seem like a total loss after four years of little sleep, no vacation and no entertainment; however, many future patients will be glad that you were prevented from medically treating them before you were really prepared. You too will later rejoice for the number of malpractice cases that were averted because of this temporary failure. All things do work together for good, even things that don't seem spiritual. God has already set the precedent that He will not send a novice (1 Timothy 3:6) to do the work where a skilled person is required. It is only logical that we should follow the same principle, even if our feelings are hurt or it saddens us to allow a higher purpose to be worked in our situation. There will be another opportunity for this student to study, hone his or her skills, build his or her confidence and retake the exam the following year. During this time this student's knowledge base would have grown, maturity will have developed, and humility will override any previous or residual pride. This set back will only propel his or her comeback and future success, if dealt with the right way.

"When a divine interruption comes in your life it has the ability to bring stagnation or advancement."

When a divine interruption comes in your life it has the ability to bring stagnation or advancement. Either you will remain in a state of fear or doubt or you will look ahead with confidence for the interruption to work for your good. It is during this time of insecurity that you are more prone to question your very existence. The question most asked is, "Why is this happening to me?" The eternal God, who created everyone and everything, is in control of all things including the calamity that you are currently facing. This delay is not an accident. God is not trying to punish you. Yes, he does chasten his children (see **Hebrews 12:6**). The word chasten in the Hebrew is "mucar" or "paideia" in the Greek. It means to discipline and train a child in such a way that character is developed. As you yield to God's purpose and chosen method to redirect your course, He will use it to develop your character. Some define character as the real you under pressure or the components of what you think, feel and how you behave. Your character is important because it is the real you!

Oftentimes, I would pray asking God to use me for His glory. However, I did not expect the manner in which He would choose to do so. In order for Him to use me, He would have to interrupt my plans. Upon completion of my Podiatric Medicine and Surgical Residency, God threw another wrench in my plans. Every door for employment or private practice was closed. Student loans were coming due and there was no income being generated from all of this training and education. I was too skilled for most jobs or under qualified for basic work. As a result, I found myself studying the Bible, gleaning from other church leaders and working in the Christian bookstore that we had begun a year earlier. Again, God was ever so gently reordering my life and placing my feet on the path that would bring honor and praise to His name. My character was carefully being formed during these deviations from my plans.

Your distress provides a wonderful time for you to examine your life in a variety of ways. Through your distress a revelation of your character's strengths and weaknesses will be realized. These revelations will foster an emergence of growth and maturity. Rather than rejecting these trying circumstances, embrace them as a means to walk in the perfect will and plan of God for your life.

The Apostle Paul beseeched us to present our bodies as a living sacrifice to God (see **Romans 12:1**). This troublesome interference is an opportunity to present yourself to God without murmuring and complaining. It is through accepting these challenges that you will receive the good and perfect gifts from God (see **James 1:17**). At the end, you will finally be able to say that this divine interruption has worked together for my good. When God placed you in your mother's womb, He had a purpose and plan for you. You are very special to God. He will hide you under the shadow of His wings and protect you from the impact of the blows. This divine interruption is to enable you to learn how much God loves you.

Meditate on the scriptures below and talk to God about what you are feeling.

Psalm 139:13-17 *"For thou hast possessed my reins: thou hast covered me in my mother's womb. I will praise thee; for I am fearfully and wonderfully made: marvellous are thy works; and that my soul knoweth right well. My substance was not hid from thee, when I was made in secret, and curiously wrought in the lowest parts of the earth. Thine eyes did see my substance, yet being unperfect; and in thy book all my members were written, which in continuance were fashioned, when as yet there was none of them. How precious also are thy thoughts unto me, O God! how great is the sum of them!"*

Psalm 91:4   *"He shall cover thee with his feathers,*

and under his wings shalt thou trust: his truth shall be thy shield and buckler".

Psalm 121:5 *"The Lord is thy keeper: the Lord is thy shade upon thy right hand".*

Hebrews 13:5b *"..for he hath said, I will never leave thee, nor forsake thee".*

Prayer and confession for the divine interruption to work for your good:

Father, there are many things I don't understand. If this interruption is to work together for my good, then give me what I need to trust and obey you as you develop my character. I give you permission to help me through my fears and concerns. I want this to work for my good even though I don't see how it could. Let your plan for my life be fulfilled in spite of me. In Jesus name, Amen.

5

CHAPTER FIVE

GOD IS ABOVE
OUR TROUBLES

"Thine, O Lord is the greatness, and the power, and the glory, and the victory, and the majesty: for all that is in the heaven and in the earth is thine; thine is the kingdom, O Lord, and thou art exalted as head above all"

(1 Chronicles 29:11).

While Jesus was speaking to His disciples, He said unto them, "But whom say ye that I am? Peter answering said, The Christ of God" (Mark 8:29). What

"Whatever view we hold about God will determine whether we seek or depend on Him in the time of great adversities."

is your answer concerning Jesus' identity? Many people have a different perspective, understanding or opinion about who God is compared to Peter's view. Jesus is God (see **John 1:1**) in the flesh. Whatever view we hold about God will determine whether we seek or depend on Him in the time of great adversities. George Carlin, the late comedian and self-professed atheist, had his own anti-religious and disrespectful views about God. He stated the following: *"At best God can be viewed as nothing more than an uncaring incompetent father-figure"*. There is no way that someone with such a view of God would depend on or seek Him in a crisis. Mr. Carlin's view is not limited to himself; there are others who share this same notion that God is uncaring, powerless and useless in times of trouble.

The Apostle Matthew retells an account of Jesus visiting the country of Gergesenes where two men possessed with devils confronted Him. These evil spirits as indicated in the following verse quickly recognized Jesus: *"What have we to do with thee, Jesus, thou Son of God? art thou come hither to torment us before the time"* (Matthew 8:29)? The devils recognized Jesus' supremacy. They knew, He had great authority over them. They understood this to such an extent, that He could limit their power, bind their works and ultimately cast them out. The Apostle James confirmed Jesus power by stating, *"Thou believest that there is one God; thou doest well: the devils also believe, and tremble"* (James 2:19). Notice that the Apostle James capitalized the "G" in God. This is done specifically to draw your attention to the fact that the one he is speaking of is above all other known powers or entities.

The physician Luke records for us in the gospel that bears his name, a story of a woman who had an infirmity for eighteen years and was bent over (see Luke 13:10-13). For eighteen years she was crippled, physically forced to look at the ground and no one had the ability to help her. *"And when Jesus saw her, he called her to him, and said unto her, Woman, thou art loosed from thine infirmity. And he laid his hands on her: and immediately she was made straight, and glorified God"* (vs 12-13). It was Jesus who saw this woman in her troubles and was proactive in doing something about it. Likewise, Jesus sees your trouble and He will be proactive in helping you to be loosed from your infirmity. Our Father is greater than all our troubles and has sent Jesus to demonstrate His authority in the earth.

Does the Bible presents God like Mr. Carlin suggests or does it paint a different picture of God's character and nature? Can you turn to God when you are experiencing a divine interruption? Let the Bible speak for itself.

Briefly study the scriptures below and find out who the Bible says God is in your troubles.

Exodus 14:14 *"The Lord shall fight for you, and ye shall hold your peace".*

Psalm 46:1 *"God is our refuge and strength, a very present help in trouble".*

Psalm 84:11 *"For the Lord God is a sun and shield: the Lord will give grace and glory: no good thing will he withhold from them that walk uprightly".*

Psalm 91:9-10 *"Because thou hast made the Lord, which is my refuge, even the most High, thy habitation; There shall no evil befall thee, neither shall any plague come nigh thy dwelling".*

Jeremiah 32:17 *"Ah Lord God! behold, thou hast made the heaven and the earth by thy great power and stretched out arm, and there is nothing too hard for thee:"*

Isaiah 40:29 *"He giveth power to the faint; and to them that have no might he increaseth strength".*

Isaiah 43:2 *"When thou passest through the waters, I will be with thee; and through the rivers, they shall not overflow thee: when thou walkest through the fire, thou shalt not be burned; neither shall the flame kindle upon thee".*

Luke 1:37 *"For with God nothing shall be impossible".*

Colossians 1:16 *"For by him were all things created, that are in heaven, and that are in earth, visible and invisible, whether they be thrones, or dominions, or principalities, or powers: all things were created by him, and for him:"*

1 John 4:4 *"Ye are of God, little children, and have overcome them: because greater is he that is in you, than he that is in the world".*

The above scriptures penned by holy men through God's direction reflect who God is when we are in trouble. It has been said that the scriptures always support one another in various locations throughout the Bible. We can clearly see that the scriptures from the Old Testament, Psalms, and the New Testament support each other in the character and nature of God. If this is your God, then God is above your trial and can be trusted? The Lord revealed His name when He spoke to Moses in the burning bush as, *"I am that I am"* (see **Exodus 3:14**). Even as God made His name clear to Moses, He also wants to reveal another facet of His character to you today! Furthermore, He wants to remind you that He is the God you need, for whatever issues are confronting you.

Prayer and confession to know who God is:
God, I ask you to reveal yourself to me as you did Moses. I acknowledge that I don't know you, as I should. I want

to be able to confidently say that I believe that Jesus Christ is in me and with me. Please help me to know you and to rely on you in my troubles. I confess that I will lay the scriptures to heart and I will search your word to better know you for myself. I trust you to show me that you are God over my current divine interruption. Amen.

6

CHAPTER SIX

ENCOURAGE YOURSELF IN YOUR DISTRESS

"David was greatly distressed: for the people spake of stoning him... but David encouraged himself in the Lord his God"

(1 Samuel 30:1-6).

While David was assisting the Philistines against King Saul, the Amalekites invaded Ziglag and burned it with fire. To make matters worst, they took captive the children and the women, including David's wives. David was not just distressed, but greatly distressed. This means he was suffering from severe anxiety, strain, and sorrow to the point of feeling pain. In short, David was stressed out! He was presented with a choice: remain distressed or become stress free. David chose to encourage himself by making the decision to see God bigger than his current predicament. As a result, he became confident and hopeful that the divine interruption would not have the ability to paralyze him. David opted to fix his focus on God and was able to lift himself up from his despair and enquire of the Lord regarding what to do. Through prayer, David was able to quiet his fears and stress. It is through communication with the Lord that we are able to get His instructions to navigate our divine interruption. David began to sense the presence of God's peace and could now remember God's track record throughout his life. Armed with confidence and a word from his God, David not only was able to pursue the enemy, but he recovered all (see **1 Samuel 30:8-19**). There was no harm to his wives or children. God proved himself strong in David's distress and He will also be strong in your distress.

"It is through communication with the Lord that we are able to get His instructions to navigate our divine interruption."

David was not only a man after God's own heart; he was one that was continually in one distress after another. He had many challenges as he sought to escape the jealousy, accusations and the javelin of King Saul. At every turn, whether in the mountains, valleys, and caves or on the battlefield David had to deliberately avoid any opportunity for a confrontation with King Saul. David respected the office of king as well as the fact that King Saul was anointed by God. As a result, he had great respect for King Saul and refused to take his life when he had opportunity. Again, David encouraged himself by writing psalms and hymns to keep his mind on the Lord. In Psalm 18, David declares his dependency on the Lord. *"The Lord is my rock, and my fortress, and my deliverer; my God, my strength, in whom I will trust; my buckler, and the horn of my salvation, and my high tower. I will call upon the Lord, who is worthy to be praised: so shall I be saved from mine enemies. The sorrows of death compassed me, and the floods of ungodly men made me afraid. The sorrows of hell compassed me about: the snares of death prevented me. In my distress I called upon the Lord, and cried unto my God: he heard my voice out of his temple, and my cry came before him, even into his ears"* (Psalm 18:2-6). He further proclaims God's faithfulness to help us when we keep our mind on things above. *"He delivered me from my strong enemy, and from them which hated me: for they were too strong for me. They prevented me in the day of my calamity: but the Lord was my stay. He brought me forth also into a large place; he delivered me, because he delighted in me. The Lord rewarded me according to my righteousness; according to the cleanness of my hands hath he recompensed me. For I have kept the ways of the Lord, and have not wickedly departed from my God"* (Psalm 18:17-21). David found that keeping the ways of the Lord was the secret to handling the distress from a divine interruption.

You too must choose to follow in David's footsteps and encourage yourself when you are in a stressful situation. Otherwise, you will become paralyzed with fear, depression and mental anguish. Don't always expect others to encourage you! You are the best person to encourage yourself. Remind yourself, even as David did, God did not bring me this far to leave me. Keep in mind; your tomorrow will be better than whatever you are struggling with today. Be determined to allow the word of God to quiet your restless mind. Turn to prayer, and you will be able to quiet the voices that flood your thoughts and taunt you that your situation is hopeless. Speak truthfully and openly to God about your fears and concerns. Don't hold anything back. God is waiting with a listening ear to hear from you. While the prophet Jeremiah was in prison, he encouraged the people to call to God with the following words. *"Call unto me, I will answer thee, and shew thee great and mighty things which thou knowest not"* (Jeremiah 33:3). Even in prison, Jeremiah knew that there was nothing too hard for God when he was instructed by God to buy a property. Likewise, your distress is not too hard for God (see **Jeremiah 32:17**). Hallelujah!

Use the scriptures from the Psalm that were penned by King David to encourage yourself. If it worked for David, it will work for you!

Psalm 13:6 *"I will sing unto the Lord, because he hath dealt bountifully with me".*

Psalm 23:1 *"The Lord is my shepherd I shall not want".*

Psalm 28:7a *"The Lord is my strength and my shield; my heart trusted in him, I am helped:"*

Psalm 32:7 *"Thou art my hiding place; thou shalt preserve me from trouble;"*

Psalm 34:19 *"Many are the afflictions of the righteous: but the Lord delivereth him out of them all".*

Psalm 91:10 *"There shall no evil befall thee, neither shall any plague come nigh thy dwelling".*

Psalm 118:21 *"I will praise thee: for thou hast heard me, and art become my salvation".*

Psalm 138:7a *"Though I walk in the midst of trouble, thou wilt revive me:"*

Prayer and confession to encourage yourself in your distress:

Father, I've listened to the adversary whisper lies in my ears and was slow to agree with you. I ask you to forgive me for entertaining a depressive mindset. You are my shepherd who shields, protects and leads me out into green pastures. I am preserved in my distress. Lord, I believe you will deliver me out of all my troubles. I confess today that I am encouraged and not discouraged. Amen.

7

CHAPTER SEVEN

LOOK BEYOND YOUR DIVINE INTERRUPTION

"Looking unto Jesus the author and finisher of our faith; who for the joy that was set before him endured the cross, despising the shame, and is set down at the right hand of the throne of God"

(Hebrews 12:2).

The Epistle to the Hebrews admonishes God's children to look beyond their divine interruption, and see the power of Christ to triumph over it. Often we concentrate on the problem more than the solution. As stated earlier, an interruption is usually something that is beyond your control. It requires a supernatural intervention. This can only occur when Jesus Christ intervenes. During a divine interruption, a Christian must purposely determine to agree with God's word despite what the natural senses present. Our thinking is the one aspect that speaks the loudest to us when we are in an emotionally charged conflict. Scriptures warn us to guard against our thoughts running away with us. This is what the Bible refers to as "vain imaginations" (**2 Corinthians 10:5**). It is almost as if you were in a sea of words. The waves of negative words continually crash into your mind from every angle almost drowning you with each incoming wave.

A Biblical example of this is when the Apostle Peter asked Jesus to invite him to walk on the water towards Him. The Apostle Peter was able to walk on the water when he allowed the word that Jesus spoke to him to dominate all of his senses. Whenever the Apostle Peter allowed his eyes to focus on the boisterous waves, he began to sink because of his doubt. Dear Reader: you don't have to sink in your issues today! Good is going to come out of your temporary affliction if you endure the current challenges as a good soldier for Christ.

When the word Christ speaks to us is received, it acts like a life jacket we grab hold to; with that word, we can float or walk to safety. It is the life jacket of the word of God that enables you to cast down every imagination that seeks to exalt itself against the knowledge of God.

Make up your mind today to look beyond your trials and see Jesus. I recalled a time in my life that I had to abandon what I thought I knew and look to Jesus as the author and finisher of my faith. I was scheduled to take a seven-part test called the medical boards. Somehow in the middle of summer a few days before the test, I had flu like symptoms. As a result, I felt tired, sleepy, weak and unable to review any study materials.

"Make up your mind today to look beyond your trials and see Jesus"

My initial response created fear and anxiety. If I couldn't take this test or if I failed, I would have to wait another year to retake it. This would delay my ability to apply for a podiatric residency program. I did the only thing I could do, I cried out to God in prayer. God reminded me that He has never failed a test. His instructions were for me to circle or write the answers He impressed upon me for each section of the test. I showed up for the test in New York with a heavy sweater and pencils in hand. Holy Spirit guided me and I managed to get through the two days of testing. After a month had passed, the results came back. I had passed all seven sections of the medical boards. All I could do was cry and give God thanks. I was the first person in my family to go to college and now I would become the only professional person in my family. Yes, you too must look beyond your trials and see Jesus. Nothing can be accomplished without you first making up your mind to do something. As a man or woman thinks so is he or she (see **Proverbs 23:7**). This simply means that as you conceive it in your mind that you are created to look to Jesus and have the ability to look to Jesus, you will discover how you can walk on the troubled sea of your dilemma like Jesus walked on the water. Only you can determine how you will allow your challenges to affect you. Perception is everything. Either your glass is half full or half empty. If you perceive and internalize that your glass is half full, you will be able to look ahead at the coming victory. Otherwise, you will drown in the sea of doubt, fear and helplessness. Begin today to silence your thoughts, and embrace the thoughts of God concerning you. Start by countering your thoughts with the word of God.

The scriptures that follow are a good way to begin to see your glass as half full.

Jeremiah 29:11 *"For I know the thoughts that I think toward you, saith the Lord, thoughts of peace, and not of evil, to give you an expected end".*

Psalm 121:1 *"I will lift up mine eyes unto the hills, from whence cometh my help. My help cometh from the Lord, which made heaven and earth".*

Micah 7:7 *"Therefore I will look unto the Lord; I will*

wait for the God of my salvation: my God will hear me".

Isaiah 45:22 *"Look unto me, and be ye saved, all the ends of the earth: for I am God, and there is none else".*

Psalm 46:1-3 *"God is our refuge and strength, a very present help in trouble. Therefore will not we fear, though the earth be removed, and though the mountains be carried into the midst of the sea; Though the waters thereof roar and be troubled, though the mountains shake with the swelling thereof".*

Psalm 46:10 *"Be still and know that I am God: I will be exalted among the heathen, I will be exalted in the earth".*

2 Corinthians 10:4-5 *"(For the weapons of our warfare are not carnal, but mighty through God to the pulling down of strong holds;) Casting down imaginations, and every high thing that exalteth itself against the knowledge of God, and bringing into captivity every thought to the obedience of Christ;"*

Prayer to look to Jesus during your divine interruption:

Father, I've not always looked to you or kept my eyes and thoughts on you. I've allowed my eyes to see myself through the mirror of the world. Quicken me to cast down every imagination and high thought that exalts itself against my knowledge of how you see me. I willingly lift my eyes to you and look to experience your salvation. I confess that you are my refuge and strength, you hear me always and victory is mine. Amen.

8

CHAPTER EIGHT

PRAISE GOD DURING YOUR DIVINE INTERRUPTION

*"My brethren, count it all joy when
ye fall into divers temptations"*

(James 1:2).

You can easily become discouraged when you are going through hard times, distress or overwhelming interruptions. As mentioned in previous chapters, the world has many solutions as to how you can fix your problems. Unfortunately, most of the world's suggestion will ultimately leave you worst off than you were. Drugs, alcohol, gambling or promiscuity will not help you. The Apostle James suggested that Christians ought to count it all joy when they are tried. He makes it known that the trial of your faith is going to work patience, and out of that patience will come victory. You will also be complete, lacking nothing (see **James 1:2-4**). Divine interruptions are designed to bring you joy not discontentment.

"Divine interruptions are designed to bring you joy not discontentment."

The Apostle James warned his audience that their would be a continual testing of their faith. The testing comes through daily temptations or trials that present you with choices to either be faithful or unfaithful to God. The temptations are also a means to propel us to run to the Master. Weeping may endure for a night, but joy will come in the morning (see **Psalm 30:5**). According to James, the Christian lives in a place where it is always morning. Therefore, we should be happy, excited and joyful at all times.

The Apostle Paul was another disciple who counted his trials as joyful experiences. Though, he had every right to be overwhelmed and even upset by his mistreatment, imprisonment and beating. He testified of the following, *"Thrice was I beaten with rods, once was I stoned, thrice I suffered shipwreck, a night and a day I have been in the deep;"* (2 Corinthians 11:25). In all of these things, Paul would later declare to the church at Thessalonica, *"In every thing give thanks: for this is the will of God in Christ Jesus concerning you".* The Apostle Paul consistently saw divine interruptions from God's perspective. Therefore, he lived a thankful life no matter his misfortune. He made up his mind that, *"none of these things move me, neither count I my life dear unto myself, so that I might finish my course with joy, and the ministry, which I have received of the Lord Jesus, to testify the gospel of the grace of God"* (Acts 20:24). This was a light affliction, that could not separate Paul from the love of God, which is in Christ Jesus (See **Romans 8:37-39**).

Can you imagine yourself in a Philippian jail with the Apostle Paul and Silas? You have been accused, beaten, mocked and placed in something more like a filthy, damp, dark dungeon called a jail cell. Not to mentioned your feet are chained together. At this point, all reasoning would suggest that hope is gone. It would seem like a perfect time to have a pity party. No one in your family knows where you are, no one is going to come looking for you, you are in pain, cold and hungry. Thoughts of blaming Paul are running through your head. It was he, who rebuked the spirits of divination out of that young girl. At that very instant, Paul begins to sing, *"rejoice in the Lord at all times and again I say rejoice".*

How could he sing? He was beaten twice as hard, bleeding from his nose and mouth, yet he prayed and sang to the Lord (see **Acts 16:16-40**). Instead of Paul looking at his bruises, swollen limbs or torn garments, he lifted his voice in prayer and praise to God. He did not consume himself with the fiery trials that was taking place in his life. The Apostle Paul knew the secret of Hebrews 13:15, *"By him therefore let us offer the sacrifice of praise to God continually, that is, the fruit of our lips giving thanks to his name".* He knew that Christ was with him. Therefore, he was able to praise God in his pain and discomfort. This verse ought to serve as a reminder to praise God continually.

I've heard it said, *"If you praise you will be raised and if you complain you will remain."* No matter how low, sad or despondent you find yourself, God is able to take your mourning and fill you with overwhelming joy. It's never too late to bring your fears and shame to the One who's more than able to break your chains and flood your darkness with His light. Follow in Paul's footstep today and have a praise party instead of a pity party!

As a result of their prayer and praise, a great earthquake shook the foundations of the prison, their chains were loosed and the jail cells were opened. God will do the same for you when you believe and act upon His word. God is not a respecter of persons. He sent Jesus so that you might put off the old garments of bondage and put on the new man or woman that praises God in every divine interruption. Your jail cell will swing wide open, and your chains will fall off when you begin to praise God in your divine interruption.

As you read the verses below allow them to stir up praise in you; then, begin to praise the Lord.

Psalm 103:1 *"Bless the Lord, O my soul: and all that is within me, bless his Holy name".*

Psalm 107:1-2 *"O give thanks unto the Lord, for he is good: for his mercy endureth for ever. Let the redeemed of the Lord say so, whom he hath redeemed from the hand of the enemy;"*

Psalm 138:1-3 *"I will praise thee with my whole heart: before the gods will I sing praise unto thee. I will worship toward thy holy temple, and praise thy name for thy lovingkindness and for thy truth: for thou hast magnified thy word above all thy name.In the day when I cried thou answeredst me, and strengthenedst me with strength in my soul".*

1 Corinthians 15:57 *"But thanks be to God, which giveth us the victory through our Lord Jesus Christ".*

Thessalonians 5:18 *"In every thing give thanks: for this is the will of God in Christ Jesus concerning you".*

Prayer and confession to praise the Lord in your divine interruption:

Father, I've been unthankful and have embraced the worlds methods to deal with my divine interruption. Forgive me for casting away my confidence in you and leaning to my own understanding. I acknowledge that Jesus lives in me and gives me victory in things seen and unseen. I choose to bless the Lord in my divine interruption and allow his praises to continually be in my mouth. I confess that I will praise God today with all that is within me no matter what I see or perceive. In Jesus name, Amen!

9

CHAPTER NINE

EMPOWERED BY HOLY SPIRIT IN YOUR DIVINE INTERRUPTION

*"But ye shall receive power,
after that the Holy Ghost is come
upon you: and ye shall be witnesses unto
me both in Jerusalem, and in all Judaea,
and in Samaria, and unto the
uttermost part of the earth"*

(Acts 1:8).

Before Jesus ascended to the Father, He reminded the disciples that He had not forgotten His promise to send them the Comforter (see **John 14:16**). Jesus knew that upon His departure, an endowment of supernatural power would be needed to counter the hopelessness and fear that would plague the disciples in His absence. Likewise, when we are in turmoil, we often feel hopeless and weak. It is almost as if our strength is zapped from us. The power that the disciples received from the Holy Spirit manifested itself with increase ability, strength and authority in their witness for Christ. They became men who were able to control their feelings and thoughts under all kinds of divine interruptions. The same Holy Spirit-power given to the disciples is the same power that God wants you to operate in today. This power is only available to those who have placed their trust in the Lord Jesus Christ as their personal Savior and Lord. This is one of the many benefits to the believer.

"The same Holy Spirit-power given to the disciples is the same power that God wants you to operate in today."

Let us take a look at the work of the Holy Spirit in the early church to empower the disciples to be witnesses for Christ.

-It was the Spirit of God *that empowered Peter* to boldly witness and explain Pentecost to the doubters. As a result, three thousand souls were added to the church (see **Acts 2:38-41**).

-*Peter and John were filled* with the Holy Ghost. Therefore, they preached to the high priest (Sanhedrin) who perceived that they were unlearned and ignorant men. The high priest's final conclusion was that they had been with Jesus (see **Acts 4:8-13**). What a powerful testimony of Holy Spirit's ability to totally transform men.

-*Stephen, being full of the Holy Ghost* preached to the council, whose members were not able to resist the wisdom and the spirit by which he spoke. He brought such conviction to their hearts that they stoned him to death in order to silence him (see **Acts chapter 6 & 7**).

-*The Spirit directed Phillip* the deacon to attach himself to the Ethiopian eunuch's chariot and explain the scriptures to him. As a result the eunuch was taught the Holy Scriptures, baptized and was able to take the Good News to his people (**Acts 8:26-39**).

It was the power of Holy Spirit working in the Apostle Paul's life that made a difference in his ability to stand in adversity. He was very careful in sharing that he was perplexed but not in despair (hopeless, filled with anguish or misery). He was not hopeless, but hopeful. It will be this same Holy Spirit that will make a difference for you in your troubles. The Apostle Paul affirmed his conviction to the young pastor Timothy with these words,

"For God hath not given us the spirit of fear; but of power, and of love, and of a sound mind" (2 Timothy 1:7). It is Holy Spirit that gives us the Spirit of power, the Spirit of love and the Spirit of a sound mind. All these spiritual endowments are necessary for us to operate in victory during our challenges. Only your consciousness of Holy Spirit will sustain you when the job, the economy, the government, technology and your personal life fail.

I too had to allow Holy Spirit to empower me to resist following my own agenda when I was offered a lucrative position at the Tripler Army Hospital in Hawaii. This offer came at a time when my husband and I were struggling financially and other doors were closed. Though I loved Hawaii and wanted to move there, I had to turn down that offer and continue to obey God in growing the infant church we had started. It took all of Holy Spirit working in me to say no. It has been said that the center of God's will is where we need to be. At that time, New Jersey was the center of His will for me.

So what exactly will this power enable you to do? Holy Spirit will enable you to operate in the power of God, demonstrate God's love and be of a sound mind.

Let the scriptures below reaffirm that God has empowered you to stand against any opposing force.

Proverbs 1:23b *"behold, I will pour out my spirit unto you, I will make known my words unto you".*

Luke 9:1 *"Then he called his twelve disciples together, and gave them power and authority over all devils,*

Luke 10:19 *"Behold, I give unto you power to tread on serpents and scorpions, and over all the power of the enemy: and nothing shall by any means hurt you".*

John 1:12 *"But as many as received him, to them gave he power to become the sons of God, even to them that believe on his name:"*

John 14:26 *"But the Comforter, which is the Holy Ghost, whom the Father will send in my name, he shall teach you all things, and bring all things to your remembrance, whatsoever I have said unto you".*

John 16:13 *"Howbeit when he, the Spirit of truth, is come, he will guide you into all truth: for he shall not speak of himself; but whatsoever he shall hear, that shall he speak: and he will shew you things to come".*

Colossians 1:11 *"Strengthened with all might, according to his glorious power, unto all patience and longsuffering with joyfulness;"*

Romans 8:15 *"For ye have not received the spirit of bondage again to fear; but ye have received the Spirit of adoption, whereby we cry, Abba, Father".*

Prayer and confession for Holy Spirit to work in you:

Father, I thank you that you sent me the Comforter to lead me, guide me and empower me. Holy Spirit, I ask you to help me to turn to Jesus with my burdens, trusting his love and power to write a new story of healing and transformation in my life. Help me Holy Spirit to hold fast to my confession of faith, and rest in God's ability to wipe away my tears and lift me from my afflictions. Amen.

10

CHAPTER TEN

NO CONDEMNATION IN YOUR DIVINE INTERRUPTION

"There is therefore now no condemnation to them which are in Christ Jesus, who walk not after the flesh, but after the Spirit"

(Romans 8:1).

Condemnation is the expression of very strong disapproval or censure. Furthermore, condemnation expresses an unfavorable or adverse judgment on a person. The devil seeks to condemn you, but Christ has already exonerated you from his false accusations. Hallelujah!

The Bible shares a story with us of a woman who was caught in adultery and brought to Jesus for judgment (see **John 8:1-11**). Her accusers declared her guilty, sought punishment for her and were determined to inflict that punishment. They disapproved of her supposed action, even though she could not have carried it out by herself. They did not drag the man that was partner to this crime before Jesus. This is the nature of condemnation, it is often biased, unwarranted, and with ulterior motives. This is the way Satan works. He is crafty, deceptive, and manipulative. Jesus challenged the men who accused her. We too must challenge the source of the condemnation. Unfortunately, we can sometimes be our own source of condemnation. Regardless of the source, we must do what Jesus did with the people that brought this woman to him. He ultimately turned the tables against them by asking them to examine their own selves. Then Jesus followed up by declaring to the woman that He did not condemn her. If the Lord did not condemn this woman, then no one has the right to condemn her. Jesus equally is not condemning you; so don't allow anyone to condemn you.

Rather than entertain Satan's lies or the lies of others, we ought to agree with the Apostle Paul when he says, *"by the grace of God I am what I am"*

(1 Corinthians 15:10). By the grace of God you are whom he has made you. It is not by works that you can boast but by the grace of God that you are a new creature. Your old man is dead. God gave you power to become the son or daughter of God (see **John 1:12**). Your name is not condemned, not confused, not forgetful, and definitely not useless. This is liberating to know. Jesus is not condemning you. Since you are in Christ, you have been redeemed from the curse of the law. You are an heir of the kingdom who has been given precious and wonderful promises (see **2 Peter 1:4**). You only have to please your Creator and Maker, not men.

> *"Often times, we are our own source of condemnation when we are experiencing a divine interruption in our life."*

Often times, we are our own source of condemnation when we are experiencing a divine interruption in our life. I have been guilty of condemning myself. I embraced the perception from others that if you have a medical degree it automatically should garner a six-figure income. When I found myself with no income it was quite challenging. As strange as it may have seemed, God was working purpose in my financial barrenness. He was teaching me to trust Him as my source, not my degrees.

While you are waiting for your change to come, don't speak negative words about yourself or try to measure up to the standards of men.

Also, don't compare yourself to others. The Apostle John reminds us, *"If our heart condemn us, God is greater than our heart, and knoweth all things"* (1 John 3:20). If you have received Jesus Christ and forgiveness for your sins, then be assured God has given you a clean slate. Therefore, seek to renew your mind daily by the word of God, and you will be able to combat the Devil's lies. There is no condemnation for those who are in Christ. You are the best person God can use to reaffirm your freedom in Christ.

Repeat the following verses to yourself until you are convinced that the scriptures are true about you.

Deuteronomy 28:13a *"And the Lord shall make thee the head, and not the tail; and thou shalt be above only, and thou shalt not be beneath;"*

Psalm 37:33 *"The wicked watcheth the righteous, and seeketh to slay him. The Lord will not leave him in his hand, nor condemn him when he is judged".*

Psalm 103:12 *"As far as the east is from the west, so far hath he removed our transgressions from us".*

Galatians 5:1 *"Stand fast therefore in the liberty wherewith Christ hath made us free, and be not entangled again with the yoke of bondage".*

Ephesians 2:8 *"For by grace are ye saved through faith; and that not of yourselves: it is the gift of God:"*

Colossians 1:14 *"In whom we have redemption through his blood, even the forgiveness of sins:"*

1 John 4:4 *"Ye are of God, little children, and have overcome them: because greater is he that is in you, than he that is in the world".*

Prayer and confession to counter condemnation:

Father, I ask you to forgive me for the times I allowed Satan's voice to be louder than yours, for the times I allowed him to condemn me and for the times I condemned myself. I confess that I will allow your word to be true and walk in my new identity. I am a child of God. Condemnation is no longer my name. I am forgiven and my sins are buried in the sea of forgetfulness. Thank you for redeeming me from condemnation. Amen.

11

CHAPTER ELEVEN

LIVE BY FAITH IN YOUR DIVINE INTERRUPTION

"For therein is the righteousness of God revealed from faith to faith: as it is written, The just shall live by faith"

(Romans 1:17).

The Apostle Paul begins his epistle to the Roman Christians with powerful words of exhortation to live by faith. Though the powers in

"the just shall live by faith especially when they are experiencing a divine interruption."

Rome sought to redefine them, test their faith, persecute them for their hope in Christ and attempt to bring them back into bondage; the Apostle Paul encouraged them to live a life that glorifies the Lord Jesus Christ no matter their situation. He further admonished them to remember that the just shall live by faith (**Romans 1:17**), especially when they are experiencing a divine interruption.

You might be wondering what it means when the Bible says the just shall live by faith? **Hebrews 11:1** simply defines faith as: *"the substance of things hoped for, the evidence of things not seen"*. In addition, faith is trusting God completely for whatever you need. Someone coined the phrase, *"faith is trusting God when you cannot track him"*. Is it possible to trust God when you don't see Him? Keep reading and you will see powerful examples of people who trusted.

In 2018, my husband and I were released by the Lord to move to Hawaii to plant a second church. All my previous divine interruptions enabled me to leave New Jersey with just a carry-on suitcase and a computer bag. This was a faith move. We were able to move into a four-bedroom townhouse, rent an elementary school on the property where we lived for the church services, and purchase an Audi Q7.

Only God could supply our need according to His riches in glory by Christ Jesus. This was definitely God ordained. He had provided these three major things that would be needed to do His work. God is always obligated to provide when He is doing the leading.

Although the Apostle Paul had not yet penned these letters at the time, the healing of the centurion's servant by Jesus speaks to this point. The centurion demonstrated the Apostle Paul's admonition to exercise faith in Christ in your difficulties. We are told in **Matthew 8:5-13**, that a centurion had a servant who was sick of the palsy (paralysis) and asked Jesus to heal his servant. Jesus was willing to go to his home. However, *"The centurion answered and said, Lord, I am not worthy that thou shouldest come under my roof: but speak the word only, and my servant shall be healed"* (vs.8). The centurion further explained that he understood Jesus' authority because he himself was a man under authority and only a word would be needed. Matthew then records Jesus' response, *"I have not found so great faith, no, not in Israel"*(vs.10). As a result of the centurion's faith, his servant was healed in the same hour. This is the kind of faith that the Apostle Paul was encouraging believers to live by.

Another account of a person making a decision to live by faith is found in the Gospel of **Luke 17:11-19.** Jesus encounters ten lepers who asked him to have mercy on them. Like other times, Jesus instructions were very simple. He told them, *"Go shew yourselves unto the priests".* As the lepers obeyed, one of them noticed that he was healed. The tenth leper turned back and began to loudly give glory to God. Jesus was so impressed by the one leper that returned to give Him thanks, that He made the following statement, *"Arise, go thy way: thy faith hath made thee whole"*. According to Jesus, this man wasn't just healed in his body; he was now experiencing wholeness or a complete physical, mental and emotional healing. Every area that could have been out of balance was now complete in such a way that there was no deficiency in his life. When you demonstrate faith in Jesus like this leper, you will not just receive the natural deliverance that you need, you will also experience wholeness. This is the essence of living by faith. You may have heard the expression before, "put all of your eggs in Jesus' basket". Give your trouble to Jesus, rest in his ability and trust him to do what is best for you. Jesus has given every person a measure of faith, so begin today to exercise your faith.

Use the scriptures below to help you work on living by faith in Christ.

Proverbs 3:5 *"Trust in the Lord with all thine heart; and lean not unto thine own understanding"*.

2 Corinthians 1:20 *"For all the promises of God in him are yea, and in him Amen, unto the glory of God by us"*.

2 Corinthians 5:7 *"(For we walk by faith, not by sight:)"*

Hebrews 10:35,37 *"Cast not away therefore your confidence, which hath great recompense of reward. For yet a little while, and he that shall come will come, and will not tarry".*

Hebrews 11:1 *"Now faith is the substance of things hoped for, the evidence of things not seen".*

Hebrews 11:32-34 *"And what shall I more say? for the time would fail me to tell of Gedeon, and of Barak, and of Samson, and of Jephthae; of David also and Samuel, and of the prophets: Who through faith subdued kingdoms, wrought righteousness, obtained promises, stopped the mouths of lions. Quenched the violence of fire, escaped the edge of the sword, out of weakness were made strong, waxed valiant in fight, turned to flight the armies of the aliens".*

2 Peter 1:4 *"Whereby are given unto us exceeding great and precious promises: that by these ye might be partakers of the divine nature, having escaped the corruption that is in the world through lust".*

Prayer and confession to live by faith:
Father, I know that I have not been consistent in living by faith. Many times, I have only partially obeyed your word. Today, I choose to believe your word and exercise myself in the truth that you are making known to me. I confess that I have been made the righteousness of Christ and thereby

declared free from unbelief. Though I don't see with my natural eyes, I know in my heart that you are delivering me from my crisis. I am full of faith and have no room for doubt and unbelief. Amen.

12

CHAPTER TWELVE

PROCLAIM VICTORY IN YOUR DIVINE INTERRUPTION

"But thanks be to God, which giveth us the victory through our Lord Jesus Christ"

(1 Corinthians 15:57).

History has afforded us knowledge of how victories were recorded, proclaimed and demonstrated. Of all the nations, none was more extravagant than the celebrated victories of Rome. The military commanders' entry into the city, special garments, carefully written speeches, displayed spoils of war, shouts from the common people, affirmation by the emperors, and monuments built in their honor all were meticulously cultivated to acknowledge the victory. Rome had no shame or bashfulness about their victories. They not only wanted it publicized, they wanted a visual representation or demonstration of it.

The concept of proclaiming also involves praising or glorifying God openly. Furthermore, when a person proclaims an event they make an announcement, which is usually followed by a show or demonstration of the evidence for their victory. Since all power has been given to Jesus in heaven and earth (**see Matthew 28:18**), the battle over your challenges are already won. As a believer in Christ, you don't have to wait until others confirm your victory. You can begin to shout your praise of thanks even while you are in your troubles. Not only are you recognizing that change is coming, you are also demonstrating that you believe that the change is already in the spiritual realm waiting to manifest in the earth realm.

"You can begin to shout your praise of thanks even while you are in your troubles."

The children of Israel were commanded to march around the city of Jericho (see **Joshua 6:1-21**) for six days. On the seventh day they were to circle the city seven times, listen for the priest to blow the trumpet and then shout. Once the Israelites obeyed God's instructions, the walls of Jericho fell down just like He said it would. God has already given you victory over your predicament. The trumpet is sounding now and it is time to shout the victory. Just like the Roman victory celebration involved utterances that were loud, joyful and triumphant, we should follow a similar pattern. What shall you proclaim? You can begin by offering the sacrifice of praise to God continually, that is, the fruit of your lips giving thanks to his name (see **Hebrews 13:15**). Your praise to God may be expressed in many ways through your speech. Speaking of God's delivering power, singing of his goodness, or testifying to others of what he has done for you are ways you can shout the victory.

King David was at a loss for words when God was restoring him after he had sinned with Bathsheba. His plea to the Lord was, *"O Lord, open thou my lips; and my mouth shall shew forth thy praise"*. If you don't know how to shout like King David, then open your mouth and the Spirit of God will fill it with beautiful words of adoration and thanksgiving.

Begin to proclaim and shout your victory:

Psalm 5:11 *"But let all those that put their trust in thee* rejoice: let them ever shout for joy, because thou defendest them: let them also that love thy name be joyful in thee".

Psalm 9:2 *"I will be glad and rejoice in thee: I will sing praise to thy name, O thou most High".*

Psalm 32:11 *"Be glad in the Lord, and rejoice, ye righteous: and shout for joy, all ye that are upright in heart".*

Psalm 41:11 *"By this I know that thou favourest me, because mine enemy doth not triumph over me".*

Psalm 47:1 *"O clap your hands, all ye people; shout unto God with the voice of triumph".*

Psalm 63:7 *"Because thou hast been my help, therefore in the shadow of thy wings will I rejoice".*

Psalm 92:4 *"For thou, Lord, hast made me glad through thy work: I will triumph in the works of thy hands".*

Philippians 4:4 *"Rejoice in the Lord always: and again I say, Rejoice".*

Thessalonians 5:16 *"Rejoice evermore".*

Prayer and confession for your victory in your divine interruption:
Father I thank you and rejoice for my victory over this

divine interruption. I choose to open my mouth and declare that you have done valiantly in my life and have brought me out of this trouble with your strong arm.

You have removed all my fears, worry and doubt out of my mind and heart and have given me triumphing assurance that victory has already been won. By faith I boldly proclaim and shout Hallelujah. Amen.

DAILY CONFESSION DURING YOUR DIVINE INTERRUPTION

I encourage you to daily read, meditate, and openly proclaim God's word as a reminder of the victory you have in Christ during every divine interruption that arise in your life.

"Since I am in Christ all things are working together for my good. I have been justified – completely forgiven and made righteous (see **Romans 5:1**). I am firmly rooted and built up in Christ (see **Colossians 2:7**). Therefore, I am free forever from condemnation (see **Romans 8:1**). Every negative word spoken against me is only affirmation that I am a child of God. God is ordering my steps and making every crooked path straight (see **Isaiah 40:4**). I am blessed of God and no one can curse me (see **Numbers 23:8**). Jesus has redeemed my life from destruction. As a result, I will not die during my divine interruption but live to proclaim the works of God" (see **Psalm 118:17**).

Since I am in Christ all things are working together for my good. I have been rescued from the domain of Satan's rule and transferred to the kingdom of Christ (see **Colossians 1:13**). I have the right to come boldly before the throne of God to find mercy and grace in time of need (see **Hebrews 4:16**). Therefore, the greater one lives in me and makes available to me His overcoming power (see **1 John 4:4**). No weapon formed against God's divine plan for my life can prosper (see **Isaiah 54:17**). My Father is greater than all; no man can pluck me out of his hand (see **John 10:29**). He guides and directs my path and saves me from every pitfall.

Since I am in Christ all things are working together for my good. God has given me great and precious promises. Thus, I am a partaker of God's divine nature (see **2 Peter 1:4**). He is able to do exceeding abundantly above all that I can ask or think, according to the power that works in me (see **Ephesians 3:20**). Therefore, any setback or interference is only a tool to redirect me into the divine plan of God. The Lord is my shepherd; I shall not want (see **Psalm 23:1**). I am persuaded that it is the Father's good pleasure to give me the kingdom (see **Luke 12:32**). I will be still and know that He is my God who is working in every interruption in my life (see **Psalm 46:10**).

Since I am in Christ all things are working together for my good. I have received the Spirit of God that I might know the things freely given to me by God (see **1 Corinthians 2:12**). Therefore, every hurdle is an opportunity for me to leap over the wall of opposition and run through the snares set by the adversary (see **2 Samuel 22:30**). God has girded me with strength, and makes my way perfect (see **Psalm 18:32**). As a result, every roadblock is a tool for me to step up to the winner's circle.

Since I am in Christ all things are working together for my good. I was predestined by God to be adopted into His family (see **Ephesians 1:5**). I am of a chosen generation, a royal priesthood, a holy nation, and a peculiar person to show God's praise in the earth (see **1 Peter 2:9**). Therefore, the same mind that was in Jesus Christ is in me also. I stand on the word of God, by His stripes I am healed physically, mentally and emotionally (see **1 Peter 2:24**). My current challenges must submit to the power of Christ. Therefore, none of these interruptions move me. The sovereign God is over all things in my life. God's thoughts toward me are of peace, and not evil, to give me an expected end (**Jeremiah 29:11**). I am convinced that the purpose of this divine interruption is to work to fulfill God's eternal plan for my life. Thank you Lord for an opportunity to draw near to you.

FINAL WORDS

My prayer is that every person reading this volume would recognize that interruptions, which have taken place in their lives, did not happen because of a lack of love from God or a punishment from Him. His thoughts toward you are of peace, and not of evil (see **Jeremiah 29:11**). He further desires you to draw near to Him so that His presence can surround you and fill you with His peace. The reason for your divine Interruption is to refine you as pure gold and lead you by still waters and into greener pastures. I challenge you to exercise your faith and embrace your difficulties. As you allow God to take you by the hand, He will prove Himself to be a very present help in your challenges. He will not leave or forsake you. He has paid a great price for you. God will not harm you as you navigate the interruptions that seem to cross your path at the most inconvenient time. Divine interruptions are the method God uses to redirect, instruct and guide you into His perfect will for your life.

ABOUT THE AUTHOR

The author of this work is the Holy Spirit of God. He has inspired and directed the words penned on each page. His works speak for themselves throughout the entire Bible and the lives of the saints of God.

ABOUT THE CO-AUTHOR

Upon receiving Jesus Christ as her personal Lord and Savior in 1989, Dr. Melrose Blake-Bethea has lived a life of having continual divine interruptions. Each trial has served as a tool to stimulate growth, develop dependency on the Lord, foster intimacy with the Father and fashion her to become a capable minister of the Gospel. Understanding that God is the Balm in Gilead and the Physician Healer, Dr. Bethea deems it her duty to herald that God heals both naturally and spiritually.

She is the co-pastor and co-founder of God's Life Christian Church (GLCC) in Irvington, NJ and

Ewa Beach, Hawaii, along with her husband Bishop Calvin L. Bethea. She is dedicated and committed to living a life of prayer and intercession. Therefore, she believes in being a doer of the word and not a hearer or repeater. To that end, she oversees the intercessory ministry at the church. In addition, she provides oversight to the King's Kids Children's Church, Hospitality Ministry, the Free Supermarket and Virtuous Women's Fellowship.

She is the recipient of a Bachelor of Arts in Sociology and Psychology from Rutgers University. To further her education, she attended the New York College of Podiatry Medicine where she received her Doctorate of Podiatric Medicine. After completing a surgical residency, God interrupted Dr. Bethea's career and impressed upon her to build a church with her husband for His glory.

In her effort to serve the Body of Christ, Dr. Bethea is co-owner of Hawaii Christian Outlet (HCO). HCO is a Christian resource center with a mission to equip Christians for the work of the ministry with training materials, study aides, evangelistic tools and personal development resources for children and adults. She is also the chief editor for God's Life Publishing, which is a ministry of GLCC to assist Christian authors to publish their books.

Contact The Co-Author

Email: melrosedpm@verizon.net

Other Helpful links

hawaiichristianoutlet.com
godslifeonline.org

It's finally here!
The **"one-book-fits-all Christians"** has arrived.

* It's a book and a workbook in one.
* A Christian, multi-purpose manual.
* It is being used in a variety of settings:

*Personal Study,
*Small Group,
*Cell Group,
*Ministry and Church
*Bible Studies.
*New Converts Classes,
*New Members Classes,
*Men's Fellowship,
*Women's Fellowship,
*Sunday School Classes,
*Youth Bible Study,
*Church Plant Bible Study
*Christian School Curriculum

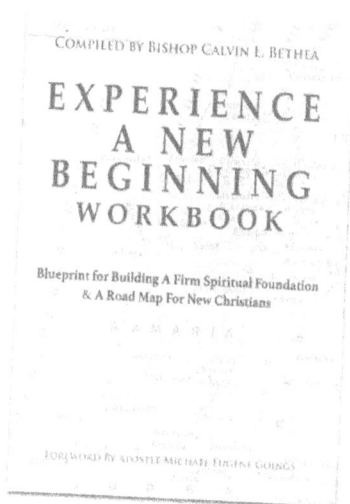

COMPILED BY BISHOP CALVIN L. BETHEA

EXPERIENCE
A NEW
BEGINNING
WORKBOOK

Blueprint for Building A Firm Spiritual Foundation
& A Road Map For New Christians

FOREWORD BY APOSTLE MICHAEL EUGENE GOINGS

*Finally, here's a book
for every Christian
at all levels of
spiritual maturity!*

God's Life
PUBLISHING
www.godslifepublishing.org

Availiable at:
your local Christian Bookstore
or visit us at
godslifepublishing.org
for store information

Distributed by:
Anchor Distributors

www.ingramcontent.com/pod-product-compliance
Lightning Source LLC
Chambersburg PA
CBHW061242060425
24668CB00014B/1246